VISIBLE HEAVENS

Visible Heavens

Poems by

Joanna Solfrian

The Kent State University Press

Kent, Ohio

© 2010 by Joanna Solfrian
Library of Congress Catalog Card Number 2010020016
ISBN 978-1-60635-066-9
Manufactured in the United States of America

The Wick Poetry Series is sponsored by the Stan and Tom Wick Poetry Center and the Department of English at Kent State University.

Library of Congress Cataloging-in-Publication Data
Solfrian, Joanna, 1973–
    Visible heavens : poems / by Joanna Solfrian.
        p.   cm. — (Wick poetry first book series)
    ISBN 978-1-60635-066-9 (pbk. : alk. paper) ∞
    I. Title.
    PS3619.O43254V57 2010
    813'.6—dc22   2010020016

British Library Cataloging-in-Publication data are available.

14 13 12 11 10   5 4 3 2 1

for my true blue, Scott,

and for my mother,

Janet King Marsden

CONTENTS

ACKNOWLEDGMENTS

Grateful acknowledgement is made to the editors of those publications in which the following poems, sometimes in different form, originally appeared:

The Amherst Review	"Ode to My Thigh"
bigcitylit.com	"Dialogue"
	"First Snowstorm, 2003"
	"Otherworld"
Image	"The Priest Stops in the Church- yard"
	"I Used to Light Candles for You"
Margie	"To a Friend"
Pleiades	"Sometimes a Gray Mood Comes"
Rattapallax	"Meditation in a Waiting Room"
	"You Among Stones"
The Saranac Review	"Morning"
Shade 2006	"Poetry"
	"A Dream in Four Parts"
The Southern Review	"December 15, 2004"
The Spoon River Poetry Review	"We Arrive Home After a Film"
The Timber Creek Review	"The Imagination Pictures Emily with Children"

Many thanks to my manuscript critics, who chose to read my work when they could have been writing: Jill DiDonato, Matt Robertson, Eliot Schrefer, and Michael Stearns. Many thanks also to the Brooklyn Learning Center and to my students who let me miss work to do poetry things. To my mentors, Dennis Nurkse, Dzvinia Orlowsky, and Baron Wormser; your hearts are as giant as your egos are small. Thanks to my MacDowell friends Olivia Gentile and Julian Rubinstein, who, aside from providing good conversation, tapped the reptilian brain with gym visits and ping-pong. And warm respect to my sanctuaries, the MacDowell Colony and the Stonecoast MFA Program.

Sometimes the last reader for any group of manuscripts feels a swoon coming on—so many strong voices right in front of you, in various fonts. The Stan and Tom Wick Poetry Prize was no exception—a smorgasbord of savory tastes and styles. May all the fine finalists discover publishing homes soon.

Joanna Solfrian's poems stood out, would not let go.

"I've never won anything," she wrote. Ding!

Some poems carry us so gracefully into a zone of deep quietude, we must backtrack carefully to discover how in the world we arrived there. Cleanly, washed of chatter and distraction—as if a wave of clarity had plucked us from the swirl. "My Complicated Love," an exquisite and haunting poem, suggests that an awareness of echoes and a lifetime of simple, thoughtful trades, in private rooms and the wide wilderness, might be at the heart of this cleansing transaction. Solfrian evokes so many potent scenes in her often-brief poems, moving elegantly, one to the next, till we find ourselves standing thunderstruck in a well-lit last phrase. I admire her bravery—she feels no need to create exact stepping-stones, but trusts a reader's ability to leap and land on something that doesn't give way.

Solfrian has a great gift for creating space, and loss, and longing. Through the careful use of unobtrusive images, elemental, elusive apprehensions become palpable entities in her poems. Scatterings feel distilled. The silence of deep attention reverberates beneath her lines—"the presence of death in every lily / which is not the whole of the lily, / but something of it." Passion and solitude are shaken together in a rich mix.

She seems like someone you'd hope to be seated next to on a long flight.

"I want to hear your list of tragedies. We'll see whose is longer." Her low thrum of melancholy sparked with wit establishes a comfortable field of exchange—"I sing 'Panis Angelicus' like someone being forced / to sing 'Panis Angelicus.'" Her missing of a gone mother will resonate in profound ways for all who have lost precious loved ones. There is ongoing grief, and a pungent sense of daily pleasure, intertwined and richly mingled. We are rescued by the pleasure of thinking, through conversations with ourselves, and simple, startling lines. The narrative prose poem "December 15, 2004" describing a shopping expedition on behalf of a little boy she doesn't even know, and a selected gift for his teacher, is written with such acutely engaging detail and tone one might feel one's own shopping trips uplifted, just to remember the enlivening care of this tale, and its spectacular ending.

So the "heavens"—it would seem—are all around us. How we enter them has much to do with how we remember, move through the world, speak. "It is a gift, this light we hold in our lungs"—but so easy to forget that. Wherever she is, Solfrian is willing to invoke the potent presence of mystery to create a sense of belonging, or moving beyond. Even when speaking to a snake, she can say, "I am a nice person, / and not a fundamentalist." Could there be a more excellent melancholic poem than "23 President Street, Brooklyn"—its chiseled domain offering the nostalgia we carry through our days in a single, small cup, perfectly placed?

We offer up our own cup of gratitude for a remarkable new voice and its gracious generosity, befriending us, and all our lives.

1

SOMETIMES A GRAY MOOD COMES

Sometimes a gray mood comes
an elected valley in the heart
a flock of clouds—
it is then that the woman
walks very far to find warm weather,
a simple horizon with a sea,
a boat, and a shore that is long.
There is a man waiting

with flowers at the bedside.
Sometimes she returns,
sometimes he must go find her.
The sea, the boat, the shore—
these things know where she is—
as does the presence of death in every lily,
which is not the whole of the lily,
but something of it.

UNFORTUNATELY I REALIZED THIS

Your voice comes over the phone line
into my kitchen, right above the round dinner plates.
You remind me, jokingly, that we used to sit
together on bus rides and I never let you touch me.
PT, you called me: Perfect Tits.

I hear odd pauses in your speech; you're inhaling
smoke. I hear the exhale
through the static, a long *whoosh*, evidence that you're alive.
You're outside. Your breath is manifest in the air.

Yes, I'm married.
I leave out the word *happily*, because I think it makes people sound
    as if they're lying.
As if *happily* really means *we have nothing in common*
or *he can't bear to watch me undress.*

(I bet you're thinking of them now, wondering, do they sag?)

I want to hear your list of tragedies. We'll see whose is longer.

Your father died of prostate cancer,
you've had two brain surgeries,
you were in jail for a year.

OK, you win.

But, really, I want you to tell me about that day
all the rich kids' parents showed up for Parents' Weekend
and you were embarrassed by your mother's pink nails and Capri Lights.
Do you remember that? I saw you shrink
into yourself, thinking, perhaps,
someday someone will make a movie about me.

I understand the shrinking,
but we don't talk about it.
Instead, we talk about where our old friends ended up,
about how Lenny committed suicide by lying down on train tracks.
In terms of what's quantifiable,

my list is not very long.
My mom was sick for four years with cancer
and died when I was twenty. That's about it.
Dad's remarried; there's nothing wrong with his wife.

I've learned something about resignation.
I've learned to fool myself into thinking that wind is the trees breathing.

—I like to mention that four years part.
I do the math, one-fifth of my life
when she finally died in our living room,
but I don't mention this.
I'm waiting for you to tell me you've always had a crush on me.

And there it is: you've said it.

Why must we pollute these conversations?
Why do we offer the birds' nests of our hands?

I look down
at the round dinner plates,
wonder what I should cook. My eyes wander
around the kitchen
and then: fuck it.

What were you in jail for?

Arson.

Davey, I laugh, *what the hell did you burn down?*

He pauses.

I don't want to talk about it.

I want to tell you I get it, because I think I do.
The small fire between your fingers isn't enough,
your white breath isn't enough.

This is about all we have in common:

it isn't enough for me, either.

DIALOGUE

The new sun fills the sky
and underneath the earth lie the ashes
of a woman. Come nightfall,
the stars will light their small fires
and the night-worms will tunnel through earth.
The ashes of the woman
talk to the sun in a language
only ashes and suns understand.

When the stars begin their silent processional,
so too the night-worms their choreography.
Being neither of the sky nor earth,
I have no swaddling of star dust,
no knowledge of the underworld.
Time is still ticked off in hours.

What do I know of sitting on a park bench,
as I sit now, next to this old man?
He has just nodded hello,
he has just lifted his brow
to the sun.

THE BREAD OF ANGELS
Old Town Farm Road, 1988

My mother is giving me a singing lesson.
Breathe into your ribcage; make it wide as a barrel.
I ignore any sweetness in my upper register, for I
snuck out of the house last night, I snuck
out of the house! to smoke with Jen Finch.
(Didn't people used to go over Niagara Falls in
barrels? Or was that just in *Looney Tunes*?)
The round notes leave my mouth and fall
with something of the slowness
of suicide. The leaves outside the window
are fall-yellow, the wood deck splintered;
the aboveground pool sits, tarpaulined,
a monolith to the lower-middle class.
I sing "Panis Angelicus" like someone being forced
to sing "Panis Angelicus." Her back is a right angle
to the bench. I'm bored, therefore I slouch.
I beg her to play "Maple Leaf Rag"—how can
she know something so hop-around-the-living-
room and not play it every day?
We continue with "Panis Angelicus."
Heavenly figures give away the bread of angels,
which becomes the bread of man . . . I accept little
in my hands these days except a wooden stick,
which I hold only to chase a ball on a field.
It's a poor and lowly way of knowing oneself.
The piano notes descend ploddingly, the rug
smells like the old owner's woodstove, like ash,
as if over some imaginary border
there's a land of slow burning. The bookcase looms
behind me like the medieval iron man
I saw once, in a museum: Ellory Queen,
Sir Arthur Conan Doyle, the Bible.
What is knowledge but the beginning of pain?
The bookcase whispers, *everything in her life*

has been written, though for now, her cells fall in.
A few years from now, after the rest of us pack up
and move to a state with a better view,
I will pick up stones, thinking them code for bread,
by a shore that returns after its retreat.
By your pathway lead us to that place of light . . .
as if we could find the path, or take it if we could.
Last night, I knew only how to hold a small fire
in my hands and fold a note on my bed:
In case you wake up and are worried
I am down the street at Jen's.

THE PATIENT COMES HOME

You think there's going to be
a light so powerful
it relieves the bed of its shadows?

You think a heavy quiet
will steep into the carpet, the morphine drip
will hold its clicking, the respirator
will fold its paper hands?

You will learn this Saturday
at 7:05 P.M.
that you are wrong.

At 7:06,
the dog still noses for attention.
The window frames the same dusty trees.
The piano waits for you to run your fingers
along its mouth.
And, in less than an hour,

a sheath of black plastic
will enter the room.
You will marvel at its six-foot
zipper, at how quickly
the cleanup goes.

OTHERWORLD

In sleep, you come to me,
a blind woman who maps your face
with her fingertips, while my body lies
on a distant continent, silently tethered in blankets.
The shadows of the interior are never as dark
as the threaded hallways of the living city,
though in the interior I have lost to a flood
a home perhaps, or even your child.
The plane of sleep travels so wide it wraps
around itself again until the waking hour comes
and the dream curls like an old paper
upon which, once, I saw your name—
then through the streets walks
the plainness of noon and maybe
three feet above us
the spirits—

MORNING

My heart as big as the sun,
I awoke early to unabashed daylight
and blue sky. At the kitchen sink near the window,
I filled a blue pitcher with water.
There was no single person I longed for.
After a moment's pause, I confirmed room
in all of my heart's chambers. Even
that unnamed place inside, not a single rent.
Whatever deaths I'd withstood, I couldn't place.
I looked out the window and saw the lilies bend,
and dust, held down by rays, suspend
above the road.

MY COMPLICATED LOVE

My complicated love, you're with me
in the way your eyes follow
my bottom across the kitchen,
your eyes that are blue and vast.

I leave you sometimes
behind a brick wall in a city
where pigeons paint the sidewalks
with their sour white streams.

In sleep, more often than not
I don't call out to you,
but you know this about me
and make a hollow with your arm,

and lead me to a high clearing
where all the voices of all the years
(yours and mine a tiny howl)
have called out to the blue mountains,

which kindly hand our call
back to us, and it sounds like us,
but now with something of the pines
and the years, and time.

Whose beneficence this is, it's difficult to say—
but when the inconstant moon hovers
in the sky and casts its ghostly light

on the two of us, we stand transfixed,
beside the car, still ticking and warm,
with the residue of imagined lives

on our faces. Everything has become holy:
the tar shingles on the barn, the furrowed
bark of the locust, misshapen by storm,

even the cement cover of the well.
Mere servants, we are unsure of our halos,
and something turns between us,

like a small Jupiter, spherical and solitary,
made entirely of vapors. Then silence:
the stars have exhausted themselves.

It is a gift, this light we hold in our lungs,
so we stand inside ourselves, and wait,
beneath the sky's brilliant tantrums.

Miss Moore called it "fiddle," and although I might use
"occasionally irrelevant churning, like an outdated
washing machine," essentially, I agree with her.

Moon shadows on snow, Orion chasing the Pleiades.
Sweet work indeed, whether or not I write about it.
But if I were to apply a mathematical precision

to this sprawling constellation, I would fold neat piles
of words, line them up on a bed. Make random outfits.
A simple collection of pink: Pepto-Bismol sidles up to cheek.

Or a question of four-letter words: moon fart sing when?
They'd wait there all day, unable to complain when the cat
sits gaudily on them, grooming her private particulars.

Then when long-sleeved "love" begins to misbehave,
mixing in with the duck boots when it should stick
to cotton underwear, I'll shove it in a bottom drawer,

dance to some Etta James, get drunk on wine.
Saturate my bra. Wallow in my own blessed
irrelevance, in my own sweat, that other form of crying.

I can't help but think of eels, tiny electric eels; that's what blood starts to feel like in these places: silvery, amped up, and flashing, as if the legions of swishing tails have become such a blood-blur that the ordinary roundness of cells is dopey by comparison, a dull thought, a slow stupidity. Then there's the liquid blue light spilling from the fluorescents, dryly washing the scarf rainbows, the leather gloves lined with this year's fur—o, the shiny lives of gloves!—the display boxes wrapped in red and green paper and my god, if I could just find the rotating jewelry stand or the sunglasses rack then maybe I could get a decent reflection, not out of narcissism but out of a desperation to remember my face among these racks and racks of pants—juniors pants, misses pants, clearance pants—I am standing in the Marshalls in Watertown, Connecticut, with an Operation Santa letter in my hand. "Dear Santa," it reads. "My name is Matthew. I would like Yugioh cards, the game cube game Bloody Wars, a bean bag, something for Miss Stone, and whatever else you think I deserve. Love, Matthew." The rest of the list I have taken care of—the animation trading cards, a different game cube game rated E for Everyone, and even the beanbag, a giant red pleather ball that will probably leak noxious beans in a month. I am here for Miss Stone. Who is Miss Stone? Matthew's teacher, I suppose. What woman is this, who teaches third grade in the Bronx? Does she show up early, while the janitor is still buffing the hallways?—Now the perfume section, flowers wrapped in cellophane. How old are you, Miss Stone? Are you a twenty-two-year-old, right out of college, with inexpensive, fashionable clothes and a heart not yet capsized? Or maybe you're older. God forbid, I think of your breasts. Are they low and pendulous, have your bra straps made permanent dents in your shoulders? Maybe you're from the Bronx. Maybe you're Hispanic or black. Would we have coffee? Oh god, maybe you'd think I was ridiculous. A thirty-one-year-old white woman with five pairs of red shoes in her closet. Miss Stone, Miss Stone. When you're held up to the light are there tiny holes in your surface where seawater came through? The shameful thought breeches: black women love lotion. That college break when I worked at Victoria's Secret, most of the women who bought the lotion were black. But then again, most of the customers were black, so it probably follows that the women buying lotion were, too. (Why *wouldn't* the laws of probability apply in the silken world of camisoles?) I can get you a nicer present if I go over to the sale rack. I look at the handbags, imagine your tissues and lipstick and odds and ends—how much do you carry with you? How many pockets do you need to stow things away? Where do you hide the expired driver's license from when you were still round in the cheek? Where did you tuck the clipped braid from your first haircut, the old lover's phone number? Nothing seems right. This one's too large and the leather is mealy, that one's a desperate barfly bag. How much time has passed? I am too short to see beyond the racks, beyond the glass doors to catch a scrap of sky, maybe a furl of purple light, the kind that is a five-minute gift. My hand lands on a pink bag with a designer tag. I don't care about the tag, or OK, fine, I do, but mostly I care about the pink: it is as pink as pink gets, sea rose pink, open-mouth pink, the pink of a scalded palm, so I hand over the twenty-nine dollars and the world becomes what it always has been, a world of hurt and love, and my heart swells with the thought that, with a wrinkle of the universe we could meet at a bus stop one day, me with no notebook in hand and you with a pink bag on your lap, and we will strike up a conversation about the war or the weather or what little kids are like when they're sleepy—but I pause for the electric eye to open the glass doors. I know this will never happen, Miss Stone. When the suction of wind sends me into the parking lot the light is gatherless and gray. The sedans are lined up like patient horses, and I realize it's not snow on the pavement, it's only last week's salt. I tighten my jacket around my throat and get into my Volkswagen and start to cry. If a savior did come into the world all those years ago, born for everyone, he still wouldn't have heard the voice, barely louder than a whisper, say Merry Christmas, Watertown, Merry Christmas, Miss Stone, a sweet little boy wanted you to have something to open.

SPRING COMES TO MOTHER
CABRINI PARK

The daffodils have not been told
of prisoners of war
or of envelopes in the mailbox:
long, thin breaths.

They have no need to count heartbeats,
knowing only how to score
the swollen peat
of a former spring.

Beside the untenanted swings, it is nearly impossible
to love the simplicity of crumb,
then bird,

for on another curve of the world,
a child wanders the streets, trailing
a glass-eyed doll,

and blast-holes double as graves.
It is nearly impossible not to admire the efficiency.

But night, as it falls, will bless that earth, too;
while here, nervous for blessings,
we ask for the sleep

of the dead—
just the sleep—

the lidless eyes of the Madonnas fill with rain.

EVOLUTION

Because cells split in the womb, we are made of divided parts.
Today I love him, tomorrow I don't. This is fine with me.

Though your gaze makes the color rise to my lips,
the empty warehouse still locks up for the night.

We climbed out of the sea millennia ago.
For each withheld tear, a grain of salt in our ducts.

How could I not admire all its blood at the surface?
Eve, I ate it, too. I've gone over the edge; it took nothing.

There is a naked woman under these clothes.
Under these words, a heart beats violently.

TEETH

Always the words *heart, rain,* and *moon* I want to use.
If left off the page, what remains but the desire to gnaw?

Of a thousand flung languages, ours calls them *teeth.*
But when the jaw and cheek are numb, how singular the bite.

At five A.M. I take a painkiller, note the invalidating sky.
Instead of a melancholy mouth of rain, white puffs of dawn.

On a plantation states away, bullets lie in a display case.
The teeth made their mark before the foot was removed.

The history we imagine blurs the history we're living.
Tethered outside the market, the mutt wants only a crumb.

HEAT WAVE

To match desperate hours one must resurrect desperation,
& it'll be easy, baby, in this heat. If the only way through
the sun's wall is by puncture, let's build a tall ship
with a mast, baby, to burst the first storm cloud
we see, & unloose the drops on these street soldiers
pulling on beer from brown paper bags.
Baby, everyone's waiting for the power to go out.
One mile down Atlantic Ave. the boom cranes scrape
their great arms against the sun & Buttermilk Channel
boils against the loading docks. Tell me:
if even the trees long for their own shadows,
where do all the stray dogs lie? Baby, the wind blows
hair-dryer hot & you know this grown girl
is pooling sweat in her bra. When it's hot like this,
the day is an eviternal present—no past, no future—
just church bell notes caught in the gingkos.
Forget about any lightness of spirit, baby;
upstate, there's a girl buried under a lake.
She gazes up through mud and dark water.
Children float like dark clouds come to greet her.
She knows—all the dead know our business—
that somewhere in this city a man eats
with the relief of a man who's just realized
sustenance can come from elsewhere than his wife,
who has recently died. Alone in his third-floor walkup,
his babies all grown, he sits by the window with his supper.
He rolls his tongue over sweet onion sauce,
ruminates the tender bits of meat, and heaves a sigh:
he has been a mere neighbor to death.
The sun streams through his thinning hair,
silver strands become prismatic, his eyes two small
kaleidoscopes of blue and green,
& at once everything he looks at fractures
& is again beautiful, so he lifts his eyes sunward
and chokes back a sob—now he's for puncture, for love,

for everyone in this stinking world, for the street soldiers'
broken words, for the stray dogs' brown-eyed sufferings,
for the girl in the lake with the quiet eyes,
for even you & me sitting on this stoop
flaked with paint & pigeon shit.
Baby, if you close your eyes and let them, blessings burn
like the original fire. It is no small measure of wonder.

RESPONSE TO A LOVER

You ask me why I make my home
in the afternoon.

The morning, love, brims with too much promise
for the unwilling to fulfill.

The evening seduces with velvet shadows,
and memories, and pain.

So I rest in the afternoon, which is no more or less
some sunshine, a few clouds,

grass with none other
than the aspirations of grass.

But because I am my self, love, one foot edges
into morning and a brown lock into night—

you cannot fool the world into thinking you are otherwise.
It is the world; it remembers how it made you.

2

YELLOW AFTERNOON

The sun won't have it today, anything
that resembles melancholy, however chaste.
The end will come at some point, delicate as a cardboard box—
but not today. Today, love, the sun won't have it.
It warms the mud of the bricks, it seals the streets,
and refracts kindly on the channel
and grants stars to the insides of your lids.
All day the phone has kept quiet in its cradle.
Somewhere down South a cemetery weeds over.

1.

Here it is,
dusk,

the sky's torch song.

The time when mosquitoes become lustful,
when itinerant clouds pass without luggage—

the time when time holds its breath.

2.

You can discern a moth from a butterfly by how a moth keeps its
wings perpetually open, i.e., flat. The moth loses a great deal of
potential beauty from this lack of nuance. But the butterfly . . . she
demurs. She opens for a moment, then closes her wings with the shy-
ness of a girl who's just discovered her lashes. We should be thankful
for this modesty. The gazer can withstand only so much.

3.

Dusk,
when the timothy heaves its scent heavenward
and the first star slips off her robe
when clouds pass purple footballs across the sky
and telephone wires grow mysterious.

Dusk,
the time when you can sit on a rock and write about dusk
and someone can ride by you on a bike
and not see you beneath a streetlamp
which has begun to hum

and you can think of loves in other towns
and how night is heavy in their beds
and because where you're sitting the great clock's hands have paused
for the entrance of the queen's taffeta skirts
you can love old boyfriends and also
the current love.

Dusk,
the time of day you can use a word like *vermilion*

and if there's a wind, write
the leaves have begun typing their secrets.

4.

Some philosopher (or maybe it was a Buddhist, or a Buddhist phi-
losopher, but in a way isn't that redundant?) says that joy is harder to
learn than pain. Though not to Job-like proportions, I've had enough
pain in my life to have it come up trumps. But lately I've been won-
dering how to work at joy. My sleeves are rolled up. My fingers are
willing to get dirty.

But Pain, always the ready cloak, lobs up all the old questions at
dusk: so why doesn't your father return your calls? Isn't this small
stone as cold as your dead mother's forehead? Do you know the new
people put an aboveground pool on your dog's grave? (Though even
you and Pain know that last one is almost funny.) When I don't an-
swer, Pain starts patting its pockets, pretending to look for lost keys.
Such a sucker for attention.

Maybe joy's closer at dusk . . . at least close enough to warrant *just
out of reach.* I'm still sitting on this rock even though the big lamp
has gone out. If joy is buried behind the last cloud, just gilding that
vermilion swath, it's not gone—it's just relaying its golden columns
to the stars. Then the stars will continue the celestial race for the next

half-turn of the clock, while the rest of us sleep. Or love. Or in our
sleep, stalk the whispers of the stars.

5.

Each day there's a brief opening,
a soft oh!

Pain, or joy.
Who can unperplex one from the other—
the same is felt from each mortal pang—

reach carefully.

THREE-PART FUGUE

1. Evaluation of Lines I Wrote Yesterday

When I wrote
dusk,
the time of day when one can use a word like 'vermilion'

what I meant was
I wish I could write like Emily Dickinson.

When I wrote
I've sustained losses, though not to Job-like proportions

I meant
goddammit, they're Job-like proportions.

2. Barber and Pigeon

In the Italian section of Brooklyn,
the barber steps outside his shop and swats
pigeons from their roosting place. He's using
the broom he sweeps up with. "Get out!" he yells.
"When people see shit, they do not want haircut!"

You can see the point of the man, for whom
every day is streaked with sour white spray.
And you can see the point of the pigeon,
who wants only a small place to arrange his wings.
When it comes to desire, can one discern
man from pigeon?

3. Evaluation of Lines from Barber and Pigeon

(I can't stand all this metacognition.
I can't stand that I just used the word *metacognition,*
and thus have just demonstrated metacognition.)

Where are the temporary angels,
not the ones in museum paintings, but the ones
who walk the dusk in street clothes?
I'm told the world
is positively bursting with them.
Their love is so heavy the orbit goes eccentric.
Tell me where they are—
I will wait.

SQUAW VALLEY, CALIFORNIA

When the pine trees sprout from the mountain in thousands,
it's hard to discern whether they're marching down
or standing sentry, but let it be known, they are ominous,
in the way that so many vertical scorings of sky
can dwarf the will of man.
Perhaps, millennia ago, things were otherwise.
When the scorpion idled in a corner or the elements raged
outside, cavemen knew what's now called *prospect* and *refuge*.
Prospect: a sightline out the mouth of the cave.
Refuge: rock walls to hold them in.
Now, we have windows, lit with wine
and human endearments. There are several ways out,
and therefore sometimes none. Thus, the landscape itself
must offer prospect and refuge. But these mountains so obstinately
obscure the horizon line that I can't find
the exit. The brute walls of this valley halt trade winds and sea
air, and whatever hope there is of a sightline
is lost, rendered vertical.
So what does one do with the terrorizing beauty of sunlight?
It fills this pine bowl. It forever anoints, forever searches us out
in the hollows. Whoever's grandeur this is, it's too much to bear.
Prospect: a simple horizon with a sea.
Refuge: whatever tree you climbed as a child.
Listen to the wind. The leaves are typing their secrets.
They write one of mine: any day is a day for dying.
Any day can break open like a felled apple, a narrow bone.
Listen to the wind. I'm coming home.

THE VISIT
St. Petersburg, Florida

I asked to see your heart and you held it out
in your palm
It was a fine specimen
red and beating with the wingspan of an egret

It beat for the dark-haired woman
who sat in a café mourning with her wine
and with her expansive gaze
It beat for the dwarf in the bungalow
between the great high rises
who nightly reads of insurrections
and it beat for the self who wanted to be holier
than its wanton desires of knees and lips

The palm trees measured the speed of clouds
The sun traveled its natural order
from high in the noon sky
to ladling reddened water
and the first pale stars came to join the feast

It beat for the cheap disguises of commerce
that could not obscure the open-armed stingrays
those peers of the clouds
and the silence of tides was larger
than the silence of sidewalks
after our footfalls divided

A worthy man sits on a porch
his eyes dark with religion
A woman cuts her ankle in the bath
and bleeds on a white towel
When pelicans open their gullets in twilight
they grow Darwinially beautiful

and whoever has not a friend will have one
and whoever has human wounds
will be healed by salt water
whether through crying
or floating parallel
to centuries of stars

A FRIEND ASKS HOW I'M DOING WITH THE LOSS OF MY MOTHER

—I have to get those lilies
in the ground before it rains,
and I forgot to buy limes
at the market this morning.

A DREAM IN FOUR PARTS

1.

You call me from a payphone in Queens.
I can see the boarded-up shops behind you,
a newspaper blows by your feet.
You've been dead for nine years.
I ask, *why aren't you in heaven?*
Don't worry, sweetie, you say.
It shouldn't be that much longer.

2.

I am drunk in a ditch.
I am burning from the inside out
and breathing
as little oxygen as possible.

3.

This time, you're alive.
You ask me who this woman is that Dad married.
I'm too used to you being gone
to have any sympathy,
so I just say *you know, when you talk,*
dead leaves come out of your mouth.

4.

You use my father to demonstrate:
this is how you please a man.
You lift your head from his stomach,
and your brown-tipped breasts graze your arm.
Who did you end up marrying? you ask.

THE SNAKE

On foot but thrown I saw it: a black snake coiled
in the early April sun. It mocked my two
feet, I recalled awkward basketball shots.
I wasn't deep enough into the forest to escape
the belch of pickups, but alas, Nature: a dull
black, like a tread flung from a semi. It lay
on a moss flat that had not yet chosen "pond"
or "land," and as such, someone in a stuffed-bird
office had planted a footbridge right next to it.
Rats. The sun was weak. A tea stain on old linen.
Knock-knock-knock and I jumped without liftoff:
a woodpecker corrugated the silence. The snake?
Placid as an assassin. I sniffed—*hardly an Eden, this
skunk-cabbage dew.* My nose itched; drop by drop
my bladder filled. Would it strike if I passed?
Hello, snake, I telepathized. *I am a nice person,
and not a fundamentalist. You are snake,
and that is enough.* The snake was still. Very still.
Was it dead? It wasn't dead, was it? Was that
a red spot near its jaw? Had some mean boys
bludgeoned it? I leaned. Nothing. I tried to be
Zen. A mosquito bit my calf. Then the sharp swell
of skin and wind and the pines elbowed: *to know their secrets,
one must know forests.* Fair enough. I marshaled
my muscles and tread lightly past like a lass
with a parasol. A hundred yards of obsession and back
again I looped—its head was nosed under
the tip of its tail; dark laughter was trapped
in scales as silent as the cross. I had failed.
I knew nothing. *Fine,* I implored the pines:
*teach me of the infinite, the circumference of the seasons,
the tracks of the stars . . .*
and the woodpecker began his reveille,
and the skunk cabbage unfurled, and the snake

lifted its head and telepathized back: *learn to love your own private wilderness, your own naked being, your own unbearable soul.*

FOUR SHORT LETTERS TO MY MOTHER

1.
I am thin and tired
and the ground is hard
to my touch. I envy that

you've left your swollen
body and have not a brain
to add or divide.

2.
I wanted to ask.
Were you that bird that followed
me as I walked to

work last week? I saw your eyes
and held out my hand.
Very silly, if

it was just a bird,
going about its daily business
of crumbs.

3.
There's something I don't want
to tell you. I will tell God
instead. It is a strange thing

to sit with your soul
and wait, each wondering
who will die first.

4.
There are still two
of us. People say we've become
lovely young women.

THE PRIEST STOPS IN THE CHURCHYARD
after Graham Greene's The Power and the Glory

It is not quite peace, this breathing rain,
for peace requires human company.
I have only tattered cuffs
and wisps of thread in my pocket
for each soul I could not save.

I first mistook the whitewashed brick
for barracks, but now, while the rain heaves
in the far-off hills,
I see how hatred and comfort
are both cool to the cheek.

No, this is not quite peace. It is the tilt of the heart
toward the immortal magnet, love,
and even the lame dog feels it
and comes, with ribs like trapped fingers,
to this sun-white virgin,
knowing there is tenderness in stone.

CLEAVE

Tonight, your hand is a sad stranger
in mine, and your head in my lap is a pinion
when once it was an anchor. Outside, the asphalt,
the dry fields, and the telephone wires sleep
in a semblance of sleep
all the way to the Pacific.

You were sweet once, and sweet still,
when you don't try to match
the cruel world with cruelty.
We said many things, meant most of them.
"You are beautiful." "I'll miss you."
"Be reasonable."

To love is to build a house with a breakfast table
and a long driveway for leaving.
Time enough to change your mind
or time enough for longing
to lengthen in the eyes
of the one watching you go.

ODE TO MY THIGH

Thigh, you have betrayed me.
With a long white flash you have evaporated
into the sheets. I cannot find you, nor can
my lover, who's mussing the bed in a panic.
We've been searching over an hour
for your regal length, by which we measure
ourselves. If we don't find you,
how can we be sure we ever existed?
Already, we're mythologizing you.
As white as swan feathers!
As soft as a cherub!
The other thigh is getting bored.
It wants to go outside for a cigarette,
and who can blame it; innocuous
is the night air, perfect for wallowing
in one's inadequacies. The stippled
flesh, the spider veins, the stray bruise—
that goddamned cabinet corner—
it would rather not lie on the bed,
covering the crossword like a prosthesis.
I am left only to my brain, and to my arms,
heavily muscled, gustily overturning pillows.
Come back, O hairless wonder!
Who else will thrill my lover's palm?
Who else will flash through a velvet slit?
To think is to be full of sorrow.
We miss your sensual lightnings.
Thigh of thighs, come back. You'll need
a dull field to illuminate you; take me,
take these wan sheets, the sullen thigh—
each night we'll tuck you in,
kiss your buttery skin,
and in our dreams we'll deserve you.

I've never won anything in a radio contest.
This is an odd church, all the tired chairs in a row.
A box of tissues. To my mind, the word *glisten*
should be used only a handful of times in one's life.
A man is about to give me care. To my left,
a scrub pine through the windows to the street.
Who cares about the new starlet? Certain breasts
really do look like buoys for the body they're attached
to. A baby wails, forming consonants with its fist.
I've never won anything. A radio and a box of tissues,
this is an odd church. Maybe the man will scrub
my breasts until they glisten. I've only a handful.
This is an odd church: my attached breasts
and tired consonants from the radio. It's a contest.
Who cares? Certainly not the baby, not this row
of chairs, not the glistening window. Is the man
a buoy out of the body, this fistful of mind?
The baby wails, letting stars out the window.

TO A FRIEND

Though your mother comes from a landscape of moss greening stones,
where sorrow was wool, coarse to the cheek and endlessly gray,
you have kept in your heart the city's sad buildings. I know this:
to take the wrong road is to arrive at a man
who is your only streetlamp, your only way out
of the pocket of the heart. Friend, you know the road that desire travels,
but do you know how, underneath the far-flung ecstasy of a sunset,
his shoes wear through?

Music flew out of your mother's fingers, and you have kept the sorrow
of its sound at your feet, swirling about each step like tenement leaves.
I know this: count the beauty I have remaining,
and you are no better than an old lover. But when we pass on the road,
and you hear the sorrow at my feet and see the sad buildings
in my heart, know that your mother and my mother
still sit in some or other heaven, on a piano bench, their four hands
    crossing—
this is why you are my friend.

3

WARREN FIELD
for my mother, who sang beautifully

Then, my youth was mostly a hot blade
of grass about the green field,
and full I was of the hot sun, a trumpeter
of heat through green blades of grass,
lord of the warren tunnels beneath my feet.
Then, the belly was full, and there was nothing
the sun couldn't hold at bay: the distant call
for dinner, the concussive walls of nightfall,
and in those days, the Russians.

                    What does one do
with the terrorizing beauty of sunlight? Then,
gallop with a glove and ball across a hay-day field,
and when lordly victories began to bore, drift off
to the edge, and, unacquainted with my own
boundaries, extend my legs around a pine's arms,
bruise and batter my climbing being
and like it.

                    Now, observing nature
from a picnic blanket, in the slow sun of sad
afternoon, entropy stirs the sediment of thought.
To live on earth and die to a heaven, or worse,
seems unfair, given the splendor on the ground.
But beauty is too much to bear. So we've kingly
named the leaves *ovate, variegated, bipinnate,*
and the leaves—which cannot recall a time
when they were anything but leaves—
marry dirt and nitrogen, sunlight and rain,
and, ignorant of Latin, return endlessly
to youth.

What is all this
hard work worth? This endless naming of being,
this thought, thought, thought? For me,
it delays by dazzling enterprise the original desire:
if I could return to my noonday self, if I could
learn to act without a sepia tinge, if I could
merely behold the varying sun, then I wouldn't
have to ask the messenger between worlds
to carry one round and filling sound from your mouth
to my ear, a long vowel on a column of wind,
so I could sit with something of your presence
on this half-acre lawn, on your old wedding quilt,
chilled in the extending shadows of this barn,
with a notebook, a wild aster, a few wizened leaves:
visible heavens at my feet.

TO BE SIMPLE IS TO BE SHOWN THE SECRETS OF THE WORLD

It's a primitive instrument at best
(in the way that simple things these days
are called "primitive"), a dutiful top,
a one-person waltz, a flattened planet.
It can't even enjoy its centripetal force, can't
let go and know what it means
to be rootless, can't snap a strand with its speed
and sow pearls to the crowd. If it thins out
with its spinning, we can't see it.
When it gets pushed, it shies away but loops
back on itself. In moments of stasis,
it can't even make bad decisions
to spice things up. And what limited perception
of perch! Either the corn is growing
or the corn's been shorn.
Still, it sighs eternally under the stars.
To the underside of one of them,
on the inside of a ceiling,
Thomas Jefferson attached a pointer,
sunk into a high-backed leather chair and watched
the glorious rotations.
To be walled in but acquainted with wind!
I have no such acquaintances.
I know no cosmic semaphore.
I can say its name again and again,
weathervane, weathervane, weathervane,
but still I cannot understand its iron intent,
how it can point to the invisible and say:
that way, there goes my friend.

I check for those places of sorrow
the way an old man pats for his wallet
and sometimes they've gone
and I miss them

but tonight off the channel the wind
has warmed and out my window
a little girl sits in pajamas on her stoop

she yells goodnight
to her mother down the street

THE IMAGINATION PICTURES EMILY
WITH CHILDREN

Unbuckled planets round my feet
I'm loath to be their Sun—
yet I pull them as they do me
till all my Heat is gone—

TRAIN TRACKS

Iron in the metal corrodes even the leaves—
some of us have souls that arrive on train tracks.

Driving along the highway one can be satisfied,
but no longer if one spies train tracks.

In the leaves, the shudder of a train approaching,
long before any sound is heard on train tracks.

Then footsteps nearing gently—
someone has absorbed the alchemy of train tracks.

To stand balanced on one foot is to guess at history.
One can never balance very long on train tracks.

Ten miles up on the interstate, a correctional facility.
Do the prisoners despise the vanishing of train tracks?

It's an equation for longing, this minor key;
a whistle hollows the air above train tracks.

No other creature shows us its skeleton without dying.
In November, branches bow to the infinity of train tracks.

MOTHERLESS AND CHILDLESS, THE
WOMAN ADDRESSES THE SIBERIAN IRIS

It is the secret of this heart that it asks
for sickness, whether it be a withering
or a bang against caged marrow.
All this steady beating bores me.
You, however, die and return,
die and return, and make us bear
your green fingers, sharp as tiny steeples,
and your purple bell-mouth,
softer than any wind. For you,
there is no *April,* only the warming
in the gods' thus-forgotten earth.
How do you resurrect without veins?
Is that how you can offer
your throat to the rushing sun?
I know you do not have the words
to answer. I think they must be buried
in your roots. I should dig, but I might find
only my own dank whispers—
I destroy, I destroy, I destroy—
worming through the black earth,
through the degradation of leaves.
It would be a private luxury, to dig this hard;
bodily hurt is preferable to heavenly.
Shall I trim you at your equator,
place you in a foyer vase?
Your heart would still be
enviably buried, enviably cold
for nine months of the year.

ON SUNDAY MORNING

As soon as their owners die,
names should disappear
from phone books,

but as I set down
a mug of coffee and
thumb through
for a different M.,

here you are in black print,
as if the letters make it so.

FIRST SNOWSTORM, 2003

We become aware of our organs only when they revolt,
is what I'm thinking indoors with a stomach cramp
during the first snowstorm of the year.
The snow blows horizontally now
and I have heard only one truck go by in the last hour,
a truck with a capable-sounding engine—
and the light does slant differently this time
of year, but I've forgotten how because the light now
is loose and gray and tangling its veil in the trees.
The priest who sat across from me
yesterday told me that we are incarnate
and that death has no dominion. Today, the flakes catch
in the screen and perhaps there are souls blowing around
outside right now, waiting for the divine hand of god
to shape them into flesh. I remember what it was like to be
a child in church and to know nothing of death,
to rub the nap of the velvet pews and climb
up into the belfry on a Saturday because my father had a key
and watch the slow bumbling casement flies
so close to the end of summer you could catch them
in your fist or bat them against the pane. But here,
snow blankets everything, and who can tell
what is a grill and what is a small table
or perhaps an unlucky animal.
Another stomach cramp, more toward the seat of my spine,
and I look for something to fix my eyes
upon but the white has set in as a soft blindness.
The day of the solar eclipse, our third-grade teacher,
a year-long substitute who never returned,
told us we could blind ourselves if we looked too long.
But we wanted to see two concentric circles haloing
the flat brick building—light dressed in a dark mouth—
even casually neared the window to glimpse it.
We wanted to look, and some of us did.
Now, holding my knees to my chest I can see

nothing outside this window, nothing
but edgeless shadow and violent wind, and up
from my stomach comes the thought that
time is homeless in the snow. Still, in a few months,
the daffodils will send forth their spires, make their home
above ground, and begin the process of forgetting
that we call living, and they will do so the following year
and the year after that, and even still when the fields
are level and there is no one in any dominion
to look at them anymore, except the trees,
and the leaves, and whatever clouds
have just been born.

A HYMN TO THE BODY

And if I believed, for a moment, that our bodies
Were numinous beyond whatever might
Outlast us . . .
  —Joe Bolton

If in the womb two cell-arcs
leave a single spine to join again on the other side of the heart,

then this is why I ask you
to place a finger on the middle of my forehead, my sternum, my belly.

For you to know the seam.
Our love's good for this world, and I believe the next one, too.

In that otherworld, where thoughts are mere ether,
you are one half of a being and I am the other:

not as we exist now, but as soul-filaments who have left the hard line
    of origin
and have bent toward each other again.

That mouth is half yours, half mine. The seam's kiss is what's numinous,
what glows phosphorescent, prehistoric—

even if we were to bury it in the sea's blackest lava,
hardened by millennia.

EPISODE
Prospect Park, Brooklyn

We stroll through the park
watch the children swing
the oaks bow
and privately think of the hours
we swung and bowed
ourselves

Wearing the expressions of adulthood
we enumerate the discoveries
of various philosophers
point to the gibbous moon in the blue sky
and call it *gibbous*

The sunlight crowns everyone

A tow-headed boy catches your eye
He holds out a ball to a little girl

I wish I knew you as a child
you say
we would've played together

You would've known a child
more given to books and strange
musical instruments
than child conversation

and though children own all expressions
I stored up smiles
for what seemed like weeks
When one finally broke
it was so large and crooked
my right eye would close

You with your sudden crown
and hands worn by use

This is the face I turn to you now

I USED TO LIGHT CANDLES FOR YOU

for J.K.M.

I used to light candles for you
(after your death had been catalogued in the secret book)
in every cathedral I passed, most in small public squares.
Cold stone, incense, the tall silence, the hush and seal
of the door at the threshold. Though not a Catholic,
I made the sign of the cross and said a small prayer
or more often a direct address to you,
then walked the streets of those cobbled cities,
threaded my way through tourists, bought roses
from a man with a pucker for an eye,
drank beer, and once ate a cow's tongue.
You were never in those cities yourself while alive.
Still, I tried to show them to you by crossing the squares
in your assured steps and smiling to the shopkeepers your smile.
For the price of a ruble or franc, I borrowed the rose windows,
statues and catacombs, and all that was life and death
and holy and sunlit was mine, for a while.
I told myself you were near. Really, I found you
more often in temporary angels: an old friend
who wrote kind words on blue stationery,
an oboe that held a note without flourish—
but nevertheless, I tried to place you as *you,*
as you once were. That's the price I pay for being industrious
and most often unholy. If I ask the skies above those cities
when you will return to me, they answer *when you leave her unwept,*
and I think I can tell you now, under this summer-dark
sky, in the arms of my own human thoughts, that I am trying.

YOU AMONG STONES

I haven't seen the sea in a year
the place where we scattered you
and where perhaps you still rest
among stones,
the waves still brushing
what once was hair.
There, the waves settle

into their own quiet
the way unquiet things do
when they have repeated themselves
so many times they have become lost.
Perhaps you are taking long breaths
now that you are more air
than skin. Not even the gulls
can spy where you are,
a cloud no larger than a fingernail.

You probably have no capacity for longing
and therefore don't miss me.
For this, I try to be proud of you.
But I miss the sea
and those things quiet that settle
as night settles when there is no moon—
calmly, darkly,
certain of its color.

EVENSONG

When prayer
tires at last of the hands that bind it

and the old dust road
is no longer sure of north

when the sky is shot
with stars

and underneath you and I lie
in separate cities

a thread of friendship spun between us

it is then we should forget
the belief

in a single destination
in a single refuge

it is then that all else
is the property of the winds

that blew while we were here.

The lines "Heavenly figures give away the bread of angels, / which becomes the bread of man. . . " and "By your pathway lead us to that place of light . . ." in "The Bread of Angels" are translations of lines from "Panis Angelicus" by St. Thomas Aquinas.

The ending of "Otherworld": "and maybe / three feet above us / the spirits—" is a variation of W. S. Merwin's translation of the Chinese figure "Three feet above you / the spirits," from *Asian Figures*.

"Morning" is in some ways a response to Czeslaw Milosz's "Gift" as "To a Friend" is to Pablo Neruda's "Sonnet XXIX."

"Heat Wave" is for Harry Marsden, and "Episode" is for Scott Solfrian.

The line "To think is to be full of sorrow" in "Ode to My Thigh" is part of John Keats's lines "Where but to think is to be full of sorrow / And leaden-eyed despairs" from "Ode to a Nightingale."

The lines "it is then that all else / is the property of the winds / that blew while we were here" in "Evensong" are a variation of the sentence, "Our thoughts are the epochs in our lives: all else is but a journal of the winds that blew while we were here," from Henry David Thoreau's letter to H. G. O. Blake, dated August 9, 1851.